64
ELEMENTARY
STORY TYPES

CONTENTS

INTRODUCTION

This is not so much a book about story ideas as about the ideas behind the ideas.

The idea of this book is to describe and demonstrate a method for coming to understand the dramatic energy behind your story and how the flow of it can be altered to shape the story in the direction you want it to go.

This is achieved by working with archetypes. There are many possible dimensions on which to base an archetype (see the chapter 'Inventing Your Own Archetypes' for more on this), and this book is based on three. These are an element of character class, an element of story energy and an element of outcome feeling.

These three elements each have four different levels, or points within them, so that when all the combinations are considered we have sixty-four elementary story types.

The sixty-four elementary story types are all derived from the interactions between three basic story dimensions, all three of which can be thought of as constituting a spectrum of arousal from relaxed to excited.

For the characters, this means that some of them are passive, gentle people, others are more passionate and sensual, some are more ambitious and others radiate a good will and heroic energy.

The situations depend on the level of order and chaos in the story. Some of the stories will be marked by either chaos or order, and others by creation or destruction.

Like the first two dimensions, the outcome can also have a light or a dark tone to it.

As a result of the dramatic situation, by the outcome of the story the character can have found peace, either with themselves or in the arms of a lover, or they can have found a more interesting life through a special insight or a new position of power and control.

Choosing one element from each of these three dimensions will give one of sixty-four psycho-alchemical vibrations that characterise a story. These can be considered as emotional starting points upon which a story can be based.

From the starting points offered in this book, a teller of stories can, with small or large changes, easily find inspiration for their own dramatic tale.

TYPE OF CHARACTER

Using the system in this book, the first part of a story idea is deciding the type of character who the story happens to. What sort of person is the story about, how do they see the world and what happens to them as a result of seeing the world the way they do?

The dimension that this book uses to generate story archetypes follows a spectrum of social standing, with clay being a kind of everyman of humble background, iron and silver being people of higher social prominence and gold being a person who holds an important station, whether by merit or birth.

This dimension need not be limited to the type of protagonist who stars in the story. The protagonist might find themselves surrounded by other elements that weigh more heavily, with the dramatic interest in the story arising from their conflicts with these elements around them.

Neither must the element remain a fixed point within its dimension. As the story (or character) develops, it may be that the type of character involved transforms into a different element entirely, becoming harder, sharper, smarter, or stronger.

This kind of character development is important to most stories. If the reader is to come away from your story with a sense of having read a complete tale, it helps for them to read that the protagonist grew and developed.

CHARACTERS
OF CLAY

The characters of Clay occupy the humblest point on the dimension of social class. Simple, honest, and hard-working, they are the ones who tend to use the least dramatic energy.

They tend to be very cautious and prefer to enter into situations only after they have considered all of the options.

This does not mean that the characters of Clay are weak or passive (although they might be) - rather, it implies that they have inner resources that allow them to take a beating and to rise above the pain.

Such a character might be of Clay because they are very sensitive and find that too much excitement will confuse them. This makes them very gentle in their dealings with other people.

People who are of Clay can easily become melancholic, especially if they are in a situation that offends their sensibilities.

Characters of Clay are usually common people or "everymen": youths, farmers, tradesmen, hermits and labourers.

CHARACTERS
OF IRON

The characters of Iron are a bit more energetic, harder and sharper than the characters of Clay. Although they lack the forcefulness and energy of the hotter two characters, they are outgoing enough to be adventurous.

In some ways, the characters of Iron are the ones best suited for adventure. They like to move ahead but at a steady pace, and so do not rush themselves into disaster or conflict.

Their sangfroid in the face of chaos means that they can face danger without panic, and are highly valued in any occupation that requires a bit more steel or sharpness.

Diplomats, scientists, soldiers, explorers, doctors, shamen, teachers, police and bartenders are roles that tend to attract characters of Iron.

Because they are a bit harder than the characters of Clay and because these two character types are relatively simple, the character of Iron can be distinguished by a comfort with violence.

This does not mean they are needlessly violent, as they may operate in a heroic peacekeeping capacity.

CHARACTERS OF SILVER

The characters of Silver have more energy still, and are characterised by the fact that much of it is mental. They are not only adventurous but also curious, and so the nature of their stories might be a little weirder than the previous two.

Although the characters of Silver are often adventurous, their lives tend to revolve around the social sphere. They might be impulsive, but it will usually be out of boredom or gusto rather than anger or passion, being of a generally softer nature.

Because they are energetic without the desire to control and dominate, the characters of Silver are the ones to get parties or games started.

The darker side of the characters of Silver are an irresponsibility that can manifest as neglectfulness or callousness. They are also capable of being very cold, especially when disappointed.

One often finds characters of Silver in roles such as actors, prostitutes, tavern keepers, politicians, priests, scientists, teachers, spies and psychologists.

CHARACTERS
OF GOLD

Gold is the element of the highest energy, and the characters of Gold are marked by their smouldering passions and intensity.

Having a protagonist who is, or relates with, a character of Gold means that this type of story is likely to have an element to it that involves righteousness, bravery or some other form of courage.

A character of Gold is often a person who has transcended the simple class system described in this book. This might make them a more radiant and striking character than the duller types.

This type of character may find that they are made passionate by some kind of social cause or spiritual revolution, and devote their lives to this issue.

Perhaps this sort of character turns out to have some value in and of themselves, and their attentions are strongly contested for by other characters.

The characters of Gold are often found as warriors, managers, surgeons, priests, gamblers, gladiators, tyrants, kings and queens.

TYPE OF SITUATION

On the dimension of story energy, there are four basic kinds of situation that your protagonist might find themselves in, depending on whether they are behaving in an assertive or a reactive manner.

The question of what type of situation they are in is a question of what it is that drives the story forwards. Given that you know what sort of character you have, it's then necessary to decide what's causing them to take action.

What disturbs the ordinary world of your protagonist might be a restriction of some kind or it could be an absence of something else. This problem may arise because of misfortune or because the character has an enemy (which could well be themselves).

Essentially this means that the character's situation is marked by either order or chaos, and this occurs either because of unconscious or conscious reasons.

If the reasons for the character's predicament are unconscious, it will be a question of either order or chaos. If the reasons are conscious, it will be a question of either creation or destruction.

Once you know the type of situation that your character will find themselves in, it's possible to describe the basic energy that your story involves.

SITUATIONS OF CHAOS

In a situation of Chaos the protagonist finds their ordinary world overturned.

The chaos can come from either without or within, but it will always find a character whose cosy, predictable life is disrupted by an element they may not have seen and may not understand.

Whatever the initial character type, the story itself will be about the character trying to put right whatever disruption it was that upset them.

The chaos could be something physical, in that the character's environment is damaged or they are removed from it, or it could be emotional in the form of some kind of trauma or a hard to understand new element.

Like its twin in the situations of Order, the situations of Chaos are distinguished by the protagonist often trying to add the opposite to their life.

In a situation of Chaos, then, the character strives to add some kind of order to their upset lives - which can make for a great comedy as well as for a drama.

SITUATIONS OF ORDER

In a situation of Order the story is about a kind of restriction that stops the protagonist from getting what they want or need.

Unlike the situations of Chaos, the situations of Order are marked by the character's sense of being stuck or trapped somewhere, whether this be a job, a place, or a relationship.

In a situation of Order, the character may find themselves wishing for some chaos to enliven things or to release them from this sense of being bound to something.

Like chaos, the order in question could be something physical, like an incarceration or imprisonment. It could also be mental, like being stuck in a rut of tired, old thinking that needs to be broken before the character suffocates. A sense of needing to break free is the usual feeling of a person inside a situation of Order.

If setting off on an adventure, a character only needs to feel a sense of boredom with their current lives to want to get away. They might also be bound to a sort of person or institution that they want to escape from. This means there is scope for a dramatic element of order in just about any story world.

SITUATIONS OF
CREATION

In a situation of Creation the focus of the story is usually on a task that is to be carried out, whether this be completing a mission or building something.

The protagonist could either be creating something of their own or be involved in a creative enterprise of some kind.

A situation of Creation could have elements of situations of Order or Chaos, depending on what it is that the protagonist is trying to change in their world.

Usually the protagonist is trying to create something to overcome a sense of chaos or because of being stifled by too much order. The object of creation is often a new social order or a new way of thinking.

What is important to the story is that the thing created has never been seen before (at least, not by the other characters) and that this creation has an effect on the story world.

Depending on what exactly has been created, the story could easily transition into one of the other situations. As is the case with the characters, the story elements relating to the situation can always change if it would make for a more interesting tale.

SITUATIONS OF DESTRUCTION

In a situation of Destruction the story has a fiery tone of things being rapidly changed from one state to another.

It could be the character themselves destroying something, or they could get involved in some destructive patterns that intrude into their life from the outside.

Because destruction is dramatic, there are many stories of creative fiction that fit into this paradigm. War is one of the most obvious, and a story about warfare will seldom have a shortage of dramatic conflict.

Your protagonist can be on either side of the destruction, either as a destructive force themselves or one that finds themselves the target of it.

The destructive element can occur at any point in the story, depending on whether it is intended to kick things off or as a climactic finale.

Because destruction usually leaves a changed world behind it, there are many different story worlds and possibilities that might arise in its wake. Ironically this can make situations of Destruction some of the most creative from the storyteller's point of view.

TYPE OF OUTCOME

The type of outcome relates to the theme, tone and energy that the reader ultimately takes out of the story.

This dimension, like the other two, can also be thought of as following a spectrum of energy, with the lower, more peaceful frequencies closer to those of Earth and the higher, more intense ones closer to those of Fire.

Although the twists and turns of a story might see it pass through many different points on this continuum, the final tone will heavily influence what the reader feels when they put down your book.

Because each reader will read the story in a different manner it is perhaps not always easy for the author to have control over this element.

The term 'outcome' refers to the outcome to the reader of having read your story and so is not limited in scope to the outcome of the story in terms of how well it ends for the protagonist.

The type of outcome is the third piece in the alchemical puzzle of who, what and how - it determines how things turn out given you know what situation a certain kind of character finds themselves in.

OUTCOMES OF EARTH

An outcome of Earth will be the sort of story that ends in a relaxed tone. Earth is the lowest and calmest of the elemental frequencies, and the stories that reflect this will end neatly tied up and usually with the reader feeling good.

Sometimes these type of stories end because the protagonist finds peace, and sometimes because there is nothing left for the story to tell.

The outcomes of Earth are where the majority of children's stories close. Usually there is a clear resolution, the bad guys are defeated and the good guys are happy.

They are often stories where people have to come to terms with something, perhaps something about the world or about themselves.

In an outcome of Earth most or all of the initial desires of the protagonists will have been settled, making the many of the characters satisfied at the resolution.

The story theme is usually a good-natured one, and even where there is drama it is not often vicious. The majority of comedies would have an outcome of Earth.

OUTCOMES
OF WATER

An outcome of Water might make the reader feel that, although they have read a complete story, they can put it down with something to dwell on.

Water is more excited and more easily shaped than Earth, and so these stories end with a greater scope for future stories and reflection on the part of the reader. They do not tend to end in a relaxed tone but rather one that suggests excitement and anticipation for the character's future.

Often this is a wedding or a romance of some kind, and many of the stories of this type will involve love and the various things done to get it.

Because love is a feature of many of the stories that have outcomes of Water, so are many of the feelings associated with it, such as the ups and downs, the longings, the joys and the confusions.

The characters in this type of story might, at the end, feel excited about their futures and about the future of the story world.

OUTCOMES
OF AIR

Because Air is a gentle and warm element, stories that involve outcomes of Air often involve a softening, a melting or a rising of some kind.

An outcome of Air will often leave the reader curious about a way that the protagonist has developed and might get them to imagine themselves what the future might hold for the story world.

Often the theme of such stories is a kind of personal transformation, as suggested by the effects of the element of Air, which erodes and shapes by its gentle, persistent movements.

At the end of this type of story, there may be one or more major unresolved issues that invite the reader to contemplate the story and its message.

Like the outcomes of Water, the character in a story with an outcome of Air may also feel excited about their future, but there may be an undertone of dissatisfaction - a score to be settled or a wrong to be righted.

OUTCOMES OF FIRE

An outcome of Fire will leave the reader with a strong feeling, and because of the dramatic nature of this effect these stories are often about some kind of power.

Because Fire implies a heat that can melt, this type of story often involves intense passions as well as drama.

To an extent, the most suitable outcome will depend on the length of the story. The longer the story is, the more intricate the plot usually is, and the more developed the characters tend to be.

Books in multi-volume epic sagas tend to end with outcomes of Fire, in that the protagonist often assumes a higher level of power, like a chieftainship or a kingdom.

The major element in an outcome of Fire is that the reader could believe that there was another story, either because there was more in the story world or to be told about some of the characters.

It could also be that the climax of the story was especially violent, thought-provoking, or otherwise memorable that the reader is left with an impressive vision.

64
ELEMENTARY
STORY TYPES

CLAY CHAOS EARTH

1. Clay and Chaos and Earth

In this type of story, the everyman finds themselves in a situation of Chaos. Given that the outcome is one of Earth, it suggests that the protagonist puts the story right in the end.

Because the Clay and Earth both imply passivity, this kind of story would likely be one of endurance, in which the element of Chaos was slowly resisted until overcome.

This could involve a humble villager who finds a mysterious object while foraging in the woods one day. Upon returning to the village, the object turns out to have an advanced technological power that disrupts the existing social hierarchy.

The object could be a weapon, like a gun, which allows the villager an unprecedented level of dominance over the others.

Such a story could be written from the perspective of either the person who found the object, who might also be the one who disrupted the hierarchy, or one who took or found the object. If a longer story, the object might be the catalyst for long-term development of the character into an element other than Earth.

CLAY **CHAOS** **WATER**

2. Clay and Chaos and Water

The combination of Clay and Chaos implies here a certain kind of receptivity. This story, like the other three in the Clay-Chaos group, might be about an everyman who initially finds his ordinary world apparently disrupted beyond any hope of recovery.

Because of the low level of personal power suggested by the Clay-Chaos combination, these stories often fit protagonists who are young or just starting out on their adventure.

This story could involve a young person who finds themselves too sweet to engage in the debauched culture around him, and feeling angst at the thought of never finding a nice girl.

Perhaps the protagonist, being a person with little power thrown into a situation of chaos, finds that by staying true to himself and resisting temptations he impresses a girl with his inner strength.

The girl he impresses might have her own battle along similar lines, such as resisting the courtship of a wealthy man who she doesn't love, despite chaos caused by financial difficulties and a shortage of time.

| CLAY | CHAOS | AIR |

3. Clay and Chaos and Air

Chaos and Air suggests here a story that is made difficult by the order the protagonist wishes to impose being blown away.

The element of Air suggests that that which frustrates and challenges the protagonist attacks them subtly, yet relentlessly, like an arctic wind.

The story could be about a man lost on a desert island who learns about the reserves of fortitude within him because of repeated failure and heartbreak. It may be that whatever he does turns to chaos and so he must look deep within himself for the motivation to survive.

Because of the subtle, yet persistent, nature of the element of Air, it could be a story in which the protagonist has considerable difficulty trying to get a project off the ground, but which will run well once started.

The element of Air also suggests a degree of intellectual activity, so it could be about a simple man of Clay who has trouble with people not taking one of his ideas seriously, although it proves to be a good one when realised.

CLAY **CHAOS** **FIRE**

4. Clay and Chaos and Fire

The Clay-Fire axis suggests a considerable level of pain to the protagonist of this story, at a level which may leave them a completely different person.

The element of Chaos could be make it a story about a simple person who was transformed by a powerful impact.

An emergency situation in the mountains leads to some people panicking and making things worse but the calm protagonist keeps things from disintegrating.

Returning to everyday life, the protagonist discovers that this calming quality affords them a lot of power in chaotic situations. Because there is so much demand for people who can keep cool heads in time of crisis, the protagonist finds themselves rising higher in power.

An alternative version might see the person of Clay burned by a traumatic, chaotic experience and now finds themselves a broken wreck. The story could be told in retrospect, from a place of bitterness.

The Fire and Chaos here could either melt or harden the protagonist, depending on the author's wishes.

5. Clay and Order and Earth

The everyman finds themselves either tasked with imposing some order, or resisting someone else's imposition of same.

This one is perhaps the most archetypal of any story, being one of the first kind of plots that a person would think up when they develop an interest in stories.

Essentially it involves a simple person who finds themselves needing to impose order on the situation around them in order to find peace.

Beginning the story as a simple person of Clay, the protagonist might have to gain some special powers from somewhere for this story to function.

These could be powers of intellect, will, charisma, money or beauty - but whichever power it is will allow the protagonist to set things right in the story world.

Perhaps the most interesting part of these stories will be what it takes to set things right at the end. The story could involve, for example, a selfish protagonist who only finds peace when they use their powers for their own benefit.

CLAY | ORDER | WATER

6. Clay and Order and Water

Water is often the element associated with romantic love, and the three elements in this arrangement suggest a classic love story.

A man of Clay, finding that he is seen as too soft and hopeless to attract a woman, realises that he must impose some order upon himself and his own life in order to impress anyone else.

Perhaps he journeys somewhere and so enlightens himself enough to understand what he has to do and what his life is meant to be about.

Perhaps he stays in the same place to effect his self-transformation, becoming a success in his field of work or in a contest of some kind.

In either case, the change that he brings upon himself serves to change the opinion of some romantic interest's opinion of him, and a love story begins.

Like the previous story type, this sort of story is fairly nice and simplistic and will therefore likely find broad appeal.

CLAY ORDER AIR

7. Clay and Order and Air

The element of intellectualism suggested by the element of Air might mean a great insight achieved by a person of Clay.

Perhaps the element of Order here arises from this insight allowing the person to make much more sense of their reality and to orient their lives more favourably.

A man who doesn't play the cut-throat dating games of his fellows might make an observation about the aspects of human nature that we like to keep hidden.

It could be that the entire enterprise is, in his opinion, doomed always for humiliation and failure, and he becomes aloof and cynical as a result.

The element of Clay might represent a person who had been made soft by a disorder of the mind. The warming element of Air suggests a person who hardens up for some reason, perhaps because they are forced to use their mind in a new and unexpected way.

If the story does not have a favourable resolution, it could be about a person's unmet need for mental order.

8. Clay and Order and Fire

The elements of Clay and Fire here suggest a hardening of a sort, and these crossed with the element of Order suggest a person becoming a complete and finished product in some sense.

A demure woman moves to a new city and comes to realise that her enigmatic nature fascinates the men of her new home, and she uses this energy to rise to a high position in local society.

It could be that this power catches her by surprise and requires a period of time to get used to.

Another story could involve a man who had fallen to pieces, like a shattered piece of crockery, come to soften and melt himself together again in an act of repair.

The final hardening of the protagonist of this story might come in advance of a competition of some kind. The element of Fire could be a competitive urge here.

This sort of story will often leave the reader wondering what the person of Clay will do with the new-found order within them.

CLAY | CREATION | EARTH

9. Clay and Creation and Earth

The elements of Creation and Earth here suggest an invention that helps bring peace to the world or removes suffering from it.

A man who has seen widespread suffering decides to invent something, and in doing so discovers the self regard he needed to find peace with the world.

It could be that the man is a doctor or healer of some kind and only through becoming traumatised by observing the effects of some disease is he inspired to act.

This sort of story could easily be placed in a modern setting, or in a science fiction or fantasy world. Because almost any story setting could potentially contain pain and misery, there will usually be scope for a story about a person who comes to heal some of it.

The element of Clay need not suggest a person of humble origins; it could be that a person of another element needs to return to the Clay to perform their act of healing.

At the end of this sort of story the disease in question will either be driven away or its existence accepted.

10. Clay and Creation and Water

The elements of Clay and Water here suggests a softening if there is no hardened outer shell.

A humble man who didn't think he was worth much finds that a special talent of his is suddenly in great demand, and his promotion to higher social circles causes a woman to fall in love with him.

It could be that the man's life was marked by despair and hopelessness until the accident of fortune that saw his skill come into demand.

His special skill ought to involve some kind of creation in this sort of story; it could be that he can bring into reality something that others cannot, like a piece of music or a coherent plan of action. Perhaps he is gifted with a special sense of sight or hearing that allows him insights that no others can equal.

The love found by the person of Clay in this story need not be a love of another person - it could be that the act of creation they perform enables them to appreciate their own self worth and to find a peace with themselves.

CLAY   CREATION   AIR

11. Clay and Creation and Air

The element of Air here suggests a story about social climbing, and the Clay and Creation elements suggest that the protagonist shaped something of themselves before this climbing takes place.

An introverted woman takes a new job and meets a number of people who were once like her and found a way to overcome their shyness. She realises what it was that she is ashamed of and overcomes her fear of it, and by doing so creates a new personality for herself that she prefers.

The element of Air might influence this type of story by blowing the protagonist around, and they might find that luck and circumstance have a big role to play.

Because the Air suggests social climbing and the Clay something soft, it could be that this story revolves around the creation of a false social persona.

The author can then decide if this persona is revealed as false, or if it becomes the standard personality of the protagonist, or is abandoned by the protagonist when it is no longer useful or when it is time to upgrade it to a new one.

CLAY   CREATION   FIRE

12. Clay and Creation and Fire

The element of Fire here suggests an element of domination or control, and this crossed with Clay and Creation suggests a story about a person who gets a major movement of the people started.

A woman finds herself in a company of people in a healing enterprise, and her gentle nature makes her an authority on the correct moves to make.

Perhaps she is, after a time, seen as a kind of guru or even holy figure. The story might then develop into the kind of personal conflicts that a person endures when being good at what they do means less time in which to do it.

The story could take a twist if the movement that built up around her turned out to be used for something other than healing. This could be because it was designed from the start to go this way, or because the movement could become corrupt or was infiltrated.

Because this kind of story has the potential to be epic there is also potential for a number of subplots as intrigue builds over power and power-grabs.

CLAY   DESTRUCTION   EARTH

13. Clay and Destruction and Earth

The element of Destruction here might not involve the element of Clay directly, as Clay is not hard enough to destroy other things well and is seldom sought after. It could, however, involve a situation of destruction that the protagonist gets caught up in.

A man goes from the farm to the battlefield, and discovers that his passive nature allows him to weather the emotional shocks better than his fellows. He returns to the farm after the war with the belief that other people are hysterical.

The story might involve him constantly evading destruction because of his passive nature, and finding that other people get themselves into trouble through getting emotional.

This could also be a story of regret; about a gentle person who was somehow enticed into a rage in which they destroyed something valuable to them. The element of Earth might here relate to their passive sorrow and grief.

If the element of Destruction in this type of story is a war of some kind, it might entail the protagonist taking a journey. If the destruction is something that they bring upon themselves this might not be the case.

14. Clay and Destruction and Water

The elements of Clay, Water and Destruction here suggest a dissolution of sorts; perhaps a gentle movement is applied to something until it breaks.

A man lives a boring, regimented life until he meets a woman who sees some kind of quality in him. She embarks on a campaign to break through to his heart, and after a while finally succeeds.

In a story like this what needed to be destroyed was the man's orderly habits and his will to continue with them.

There are many potential story types in which a gradual wearing away of something leads to a romance. It could be that the protagonist has a past romantic trauma to overcome and needs to lose their fear of loving again.

It might not be that the scar to be healed is a romantic one - it could also be that some previous life experience has made the person unlovable, or believing themselves to be so.

The common theme to this kind of story is a gentle erosion of some unfortunate quality that continued to cause a person harm or loss.

CLAY · DESTRUCTION · AIR

15. Clay and Destruction and Air

The elements of Clay and Air here suggest a story about a person who is passively dragged into something; if destruction, it could be a war.

The story conflict here might come from the person of Clay's realisation that pre-emptive action on their part could have easily prevented it. As the story progresses, they may come to regret their passivity.

An element of Air might also suggest a social ambition of some kind. If this would lead to destruction, it could be a story about a person who had several chances to see destruction coming but chose to remain passive.

This is another type of story that might be best told looking back (from the protagonist's point of view).

The brittle nature of Clay and the whimsical nature of Air could make this story one about a person's life being shattered by some unlikely misfortune.

If this does relate to a social ambition, this could also be a moral tale about hubris and how extending oneself too far invites destruction.

16. Clay and Destruction and Fire

The elements of Fire and Destruction here suggest a great burning or an inferno.

This could be a great destruction of some kind that left nothing in its wake, such as a post-apocalyptic nuclear war survivor story.

It could also be that the burning involved here is a burning away of something unwanted or unnecessary, or even something that had to be burnt away for things to become complete.

A young woman finds that warfare comes to her home, and her gentle nature allows her to endure the deprivations of warfare while retaining enough humanity to have something to survive for.

The nature of the warfare burns away a number of delusions that she had about the true nature of things.

Because Clay is the element from which things grow, a great burning and destruction might make this type of story about revival, regrowth or rebirth, whether of a person or a group of people.

IRON CHAOS EARTH

17. Iron and Chaos and Earth

The element of Iron that now becomes prevalent suggests a hardening of sorts; usually this involves the hardening of a character's temperament.

This could be as simple an example as a histrionic woman learning some composure techniques during a physical ordeal, and finding that they are of much use back in her normal life.

It could also be a story of defeat and loss, with the Iron and Chaos combination suggesting some kind of warfare that come to the protagonist. The element of Earth here would imply a passive surrender.

Another form of it might be a simple battle story, with the Iron and Chaos representing a pitched battle and the Earth representing the peaceful resolution of the story after the hero protagonist has won.

In any case, the element of Iron suggests a darker, more visceral tone to the story than might have been present in the other types discussed in this book. However the story is resolved, this element of sharpness and hardness will colour it for the reader.

18. Iron and Chaos and Water

The element of Water appearing here suggests a romantic interest, and paired with Iron could represent the effect of rust occurring to the protagonist.

A young man who is too timid to succeed in the competitive environment around him feels angst at the thought of never finding a nice girl, seeing as they are all caught up in the same culture he despises.

The experience damages his good will in a manner like Iron becoming rusted. He becomes a trawler of dangerous bars and clubs looking for whatever action he can find.

The suggestion of rust here could apply to a romantic situation that had deteriorated or become stale. The element of Chaos here might mean that such a story began midway through the drama.

Because Water does not wear away Iron as easily as it does Clay, this could also be a story about frustrated romantic ambitions. The image here might be of a flowing of romantic feeling running up against a hard, protective set of emotions and dissipating into Chaos as it has nowhere else to run.

IRON   CHAOS   AIR

19. Iron and Chaos and Air

The element of Air here could represent an intelligence or an intellectualism of a sorts that combined with some darker elements in Iron and Chaos.

A meek, nerdy man is involved in a car accident and discovers that he has far greater powers to control his own feelings than he imagined. Perhaps the trauma of the incident causes him to develop an ability to dissociate from his feelings.

Returning to society, he discovers that this gives him a hard edge that works to his career advantage. The man might work in computer security and find himself offered a position in national security or something with a high level of responsibility.

This will raise a question about how successful the newly-discovered man of Iron/Silver would be after this promotion. In one kind of story, the man would find that the situation suited him and he did well in it, achieving both career success and behaving correctly. In another, the reader might be left wondering whether hidden resentments or unresolved mental damage from the past might lead to him abusing his power and position.

IRON **CHAOS** **FIRE**

20. Iron and Chaos and Fire

The Iron and Fire combination here suggest a dark, violent and aggressive element to this type of story. Crossed with Chaos, this could mean a gruesome tale of malice and cruelty.

Perhaps a barbarian warlord has gathered enough of a force together to sweep across a vast territory, leaving much of it pillaged and plundered. The story could be told from the perspective of a soldier caught up in the chaos, or that of one of the warlord's deranged lieutenants.

Other perspectives could be of a villager left behind in the wake of the rampage, or of a scout watching all this happen from a distance.

If this type of story was to be a more personal and contemporary one, it could involve a self-destructive activity that a person engaged in because of confusion, fear or self-hatred.

The Iron and Fire would then suggest a cutting and burning of oneself, perhaps of one's soul. The Chaos may then be the behaviour that results from the agony. There are a wide variety of reasons why the protagonist might be so conflicted.

21. Iron and Order and Earth

The elements of Iron and Order here suggest a kind of dominance, and the element of Earth suggests that this might be the correct way of things as it leads to peace.

This might suggest a coming of age story in which a person who needed to learn some lessons finally gets the chance to, perhaps at the cost of sacrificing something. In the same way that a wild horse can be reined in, this story can be about the reining in of some other instinct or lust that had previously been dangerously out of control.

It could also be a story about suffocation, in that the bonds of order are so tight that no action can be taken and an extinguishing of energy becomes inevitable.

Because Iron and Order suggest a very tight bondage of some kind, the theme of this story could be one of frustration that eventually becomes satisfied.

The theme of tight control could be used with a variety of characters, and the feistier of these could end up in a battle against the restrictive order. If peace is to be found it is through winning or giving up the fight once it is realised to be a folly.

IRON ORDER WATER

22. Iron and Order and Water

The Iron and Order elements along with Water suggest a sharp order imposed upon a romantic situation.

A man discovers that his passionate nature makes all kinds of women take an interest in him, and he realises that this is a powerful quality to possess.

It could be that he went away to a war and returned a much more daring individual than the other men, and this point of comparison made him more attractive to women.

Such a man might find himself in an interesting situation if he came across a woman who he wasn't able to arouse a desire for order in.

It could also be that an individual of Clay, Silver or Gold had a romantic interest in a person who did not reciprocate it. The solution to the protagonist's dilemma might be to transform some of their base element into Iron, and so to become a harder or sharper individual.

The story might be that a person of Clay develops into one of Iron for the sake of order, but finds that they are not perfectly comfortable with the transformation.

23. Iron and Order and Air

The mixture of Iron, Order and Air here suggests a kind of control in a place of industry, such as a workplace.

A woman falls for a coworker who appears confident and kind, only to find that his demeanour is a bluff. She comes to appreciate the degree to which men will tell lies if it makes them look better to women.

Becoming paranoid, she realises that the entire environment around her is based on lies and bluffs, and she comes to reject all of it.

If the passions aroused by the element of Air are in response to the firm order suggested by the other two elements, it may be because the protagonist of this story is highly dissatisfied with their employment situation and longs for a change.

Air will not damage Iron but can gradually weaken it to the point where it snaps. The oppressive order in this kind of story can push the protagonist towards surrender or towards an explosive resistance. The surrender, though, could not come without a passionate resistance of some kind, probably from within.

24. Iron and Order and Fire

The element of Fire here might suggest power and control, and crossed with Iron and Order this might suggest a great military power of some kind.

Perhaps a warrior rises to chieftain and tries to impose his order on neighbouring tribes so as to become a king. This is perhaps a classic type of story in which a slave rises to the place of king over an epic series of adventures and battles.

It could also be a dystopia in which a military government has taken control at the great loss of economic potential or security for the people affected by it.

The story need not involve a fascist-style government of oppression; it could be about a group of people who find themselves tasked with forming a resistance to this.

If it is a dystopia, it could be because of an imbalance of Iron in the general populace. If too many people come to identify with this element it could lead to a generally brutal and violent society.

Such a story could be written from the perspective of a wide range of participants.

IRON | CREATION | EARTH

25. Iron and Creation and Earth

The elements of Iron and Earth suggest a kind of futility, as Clay cut by Iron can ooze back into shape, and these mixed with Creation might suggest an exasperating story such as a farcical comedy.

A comedy about a woman who comes to believe that she is of aristocratic descent and so strives to take what she sees as her rightful place in society. Although she gets moved off to a minor post she nonetheless believes she's an important person.

The other characters around her are driven to desperation by her hard-willed attempts to set everything right according to her eccentric sense of justice.

The element of Creation might mean a story that is rapidly changing and exciting. Because the element of Earth suggests that the story is a good-natured one, stories of this type probably end up with a neat resolution.

If it is a comedy (and outcomes of Earth often are) the element of Iron suggests that there might be a lot of physical, or slapstick humour.

26. Iron and Creation and Water

The Iron crossed with Creation and Water here suggests a flowing sculpture of some kind, like a fountain. This could mean a story about something that flowed out in an orderly and attractive fashion.

The element of Water suggests that the flow could be one of love, perhaps of romantic feelings towards another person.

Perhaps a woman who was struggling with feelings of guilt about her promiscuity seduces a young man and observes an improvement in his sexual and social confidence. She then abandons her guilt over her past behaviour.

She may have struggled for much of her life to contain her own sexual extraversion and after such an experience comes to be glad for this struggle.

The hardness of Iron crossed with Creation suggests a situation that is forced. This sort of story could be about a person who contrives a romance rather than allowing it to develop naturally.

The twist in the story could be about whether this works out for them or if it becomes a disaster.

27. Iron and Creation and Air

The elements of Iron and Air here suggest a hard-nosed approach to a career of some kind.

Perhaps the Creation element of the story can relate to a criminal enterprise of some kind, even an empire. The story could follow a number of different incidents within this time, in short or epic scope.

Most mobsters tend to be characters of Iron; if the protagonist is young they may have an element of Clay about them, and if older an element of Silver.

The element of Creation might mean that the protagonist of this story keeps moving ahead and becoming more influential. This may necessitate that they make the correct decisions in a number of crucial moral dilemmas.

Perhaps then the story would focus less on the brutality and savagery of gang warfare and more on the subtleties of the mobster mindset.

If this type of story was not about a criminal it could be about another type of person in a very competitive career, such as a politician or certain kinds of businessman.

IRON CREATION FIRE

28. Iron and Creation and Fire

The element of Fire here suggests a darker, more powerful kind of intrigue, perhaps a story like the previous three only with higher stakes.

A woman who has rare physical combat skills discovers that some interesting people have noticed her talents and offer her a position of power as a spy, assassin or some other occupation in which people need to be deceived and/or killed.

During the course of her work the protagonist finds that she has to create a lot of unusual ways to get out of what are often life-or-death struggles. The elements of Iron and Fire could here represent gunfire, or some other manner of mortal combat.

The story could hinge around the protagonist completing a series of missions or the build-up to one important event in which she was tasked with a crucial action.

The element of Fire also suggests a possible unresolved element - this could involve the protagonist being taken prisoner, confessing to a crime or having feelings of guilt or doubt.

IRON — DESTRUCTION — EARTH

29. Iron and Destruction and Earth

The elements of Destruction and Earth suggest an enemy that is to be overcome, perhaps something internal to the protagonist.

A woman is gentle and passive because she has internalised all of her fear. Taking the opportunity to externalise this fear as hatred in conflict - and perhaps destroying an enemy in the process - she finds peace in her newly discovered strength.

The enemy could be something external that serves to represent an aspect of herself that she needs to go into battle with, representing a shadow self or dark side.

This could also be a very simple story about a protagonist and an antagonist who are fated to fight each other to the death. The element of Earth could represent the settled nature of the conflict once one of the two has been killed.

The story could then take a number of perspectives and themes, depending on whose side of it was being told, whether one of the two combatants was clearly evil and whether it was being told as a tragedy or a heroic story.

IRON DESTRUCTION WATER

30. Iron and Destruction and Water

The combination of Iron and Destruction here suggests a low fantasy tale in which a cruel and vicious person finds a romantic partner through warfare or similar.

Perhaps the protagonist is a barbarian warrior who finds a girl among the prisoners captured after a raid.

They could also be an Amazon warrior who finds that one of her opponents is less cowardly than she had expected a man to be.

The Iron and Water pairing suggest that the romantic elements of the story develop after one character shows strength.

Perhaps a young man shows what he is made of by destroying an enemy that had been oppressing him. The enemy here could be a person or a task of some kind, such as the resolution of a personal goal.

In a more modern setting, the Iron and Destruction combination could group together with Water if a fight was necessary to create the emotional environment for a romance.

31. Iron and Destruction and Air

The combination of Destruction and Air suggests someone who makes great sacrifices for the sake of social climbing or for a career.

The element of Iron suggests that it could be for the sake of fighting or a sport of some kind. This sort of story might be about a professional prizefighter who suffered considerable personal and social costs in order to achieve their goals.

The Destruction element would then come through in the aspects of the protagonist's life that were neglected or shut off on account of this striving.

This sort of story could also be about a team, and the losses they encountered in their venture. This might make it good for a fantasy setting, as the company could be a team of vikings or barbarians.

The Destruction and Air elements could also imply something that was blown away; perhaps the story of the prizefighter is one of loss as they lose their last fight to a vastly superior opponent. The Air in this sort of story might act as fortune, in that it had a great effect on a protagonist who may not have deserved it.

IRON — DESTRUCTION — FIRE

32. Iron and Destruction and Fire

The Iron and Fire elements here mixed with Destruction
suggest a Dark Age fantasy about warfare and plunder.

This story type could be an apocalyptic tragedy, in which a
great warfare of some kind had destroyed much of human
life. This could be set in the aftermath of a war in a number
of different times and places, but the common theme would
be a destruction of known civilisation.

The Iron and Fire might represent bombs, whether high
explosive or nuclear. A character involved in a story of this
type might find it an intensely stressful experience.

If the story is about warfare it will be easy to find scope for
destruction. For the most part this will be a matter of scale,
and whether the destruction is physical or mental.

On the level of the individual, a person could be physically
injured or mentally traumatised by the warfare experience.
They might even find they enjoy it for some reason (and
that this enjoyment shapes their personality).

On a group level there can be all kinds of splits, alliances
and betrayals.

33. Silver and Chaos and Earth

The element of Silver suggests a higher social class of protagonist to this type of story, which might tend to be longer or more detailed than the previous ones.

An intellectual, awkward man finds himself lost in the wilderness where much of his knowledge appears to be useless. He discovers that much of it is useful if he applies it and he returns to civilisation with a greater acceptance of his own value.

Perhaps he is with a party of people after a bus or plane crash and the dominance hierarchy that existed up until then changes as different people show different levels of adaptability.

As the Silver suggests a balance between the softness of Clay and the hardness of Iron, perhaps the protagonist of this sort of story wins by finding a balance between two extremes of some kind.

These two extremes could be balancing two different factions of people, or two opposing instincts within the protagonist, or even something more abstract like masculine and feminine energies.

34. Silver and Chaos and Water

Silver and Chaos suggests a fall from grace, and the element of Water suggests a romantic aspect to this type of story.

It could be about a middle-class person whose life has fallen to pieces because of the loss of a job, a marriage, or some other social emblem.

Despair will be a common theme to this type of story, because a protagonist of Silver will often be the sort of person who has worked very hard over a lengthy period of time.

The element of Water could play in role in making the protagonist find love after their social world falls apart. It could be that the protagonist was too pretentious to be themselves, and so had blocked themselves from finding true love without even realising it.

It could also play a role in introducing the chaos into the protagonist's life. This would be possible if the Chaos and Water combined to lure them into an affair or similar.

Silver melts at a lower temperature than Iron, and these types of stories often involve more psychological drama than violence.

35. Silver and Chaos and Air

The elements of Air and Chaos suggest a luck story of some kind, perhaps a tragicomedy. In combination these elements might bring with them an aspect of vicarious fortune that picks the protagonist up and drops them in all sorts of unexpected places.

If the Air is thought of here to represent a social element, the fortune could come in the context of a character of Silver being offered a new job.

But all is not as it seems, as nothing goes according to plan and the new job is fraught with disappointments and failures.

The new job could be a new position of some other kind, such as an inherited title or a new family role.

The gentle motion of Air has an aspect of polishing an element like Silver, so it could be that this sort of story ends up showing the best side of the protagonist.

If it is a tragicomedy, the basic story arc might involve a well-meaning character overcoming the whims of fortune after a determined effort of wit and will.

SILVER CHAOS FIRE

36. Silver and Chaos and Fire

Chaos and Fire here suggests a loss of some kind, perhaps a burning away. This could mean a story set just after some kind of bereavement.

The death of a family matriarch stirs up all manner of fears and old resentments.

Perhaps a woman who has made a life out of intelligently being in touch with her emotions finds that the rest of the family lean on her for solace and sanity.

After a while, she starts to see the opportunity afforded her by the emotional crisis: the influence that is part of becoming the centre of family attention, with everything going through her.

An aspect of playing with fire here could result if she tries to take undue advantage of her new position. Perhaps her new influence creates resentments on the part of some of the other family members.

A reconciliation could be struck if the resentment proved so great that it caused her to repent, melting the hardness she had.

37. Silver and Order and Earth

If the Silver represents a story about a person high in society, the Order and Earth might suggest one about a person who imposes peace upon themselves.

A scientist finds that their research allows them an insight that lets them have a level of peace.

It may be that the scientist was from a particularly chaotic background, and finds that the order and laws within science help them make sense out of the rest of the world.

Perhaps they were disturbed by a singular, traumatic experience that recently occurred and turned their world upside-down.

The story could be about a personal awakening that follows from a discovery of some sort or a slow coming to awareness for a person taking a more epic path.

The protagonist of this sort of story need not be a scientist - there are many professions in which an intellectual discovery of some kind might mirror an awakening in the wider story life of one of the characters.

38. Silver and Order and Water

Crossing Silver and Order might suggest here a conservative social element.

A staid and rigid individual wonders what they need to do in order to find love, and after a period of some difficulty comes to discover, whether by luck or by trial and error, that what they needed was some more chaos in their lives.

The major drama in this type of story might be the struggle to overcome the excess of order which has been imposed on the protagonist from their past.

If the Water here refers to a sexual element, the conservative social order element might make for an adult drama/comedy about some kind of sexual repression.

Perhaps the protagonist has an unrequited kink or fetish that is starting to play on their minds as they age. It could be that from years of repressing it for the sake of a partner's acceptance they decide that now is the time to try it out.

This type of story could easily become a comedy as the protagonist found themselves working to invite more chaos into their lives, and perhaps getting too much at times.

SILVER | ORDER | AIR

39. Silver and Order and Air

The elements of Silver and Air suggest a social climbing or promotion of some kind. If the element of Order suggests something being set to order, this type of story could document a political struggle.

A kindly man gets involved in local politics in order to solve a neighbourhood problem. Finding that a number of disagreeable people make his simple request a battle, he becomes a much more assertive person.

This has the effect of gently transforming him into someone else, and over time he becomes a leader of other people.

The element of Air and the luck that often comes with this suggest that this type of story could be about opportunity. Perhaps a untimely death means the kindly man suddenly has a chance to take on a leadership role that he had not imagined receiving.

A person caught up in such dramas might easily lose their own sense of balance, and a number of potential dramatic plots arise from this. The person rising through the ranks might forget the role of fortune and develop a false belief in their own ability, or become protective of their new power.

SILVER ORDER FIRE

40. Silver and Order and Fire

The element of Fire here might suggest some sort of power or control, and Silver crossed with Order might represent social control of some kind. The elements of Silver and Fire might suggest a race against time of a sort.

A scheming man discovers a way to manipulate a wide variety of women. Perhaps it is through some dark charisma or subtle magic that he gets this power, and it means women take his suggestions seriously.

The reverse would be a story about a woman who, perhaps finding that one set of charms were fading, discovers another. She may have the wit to intuit a higher order of patterns in human relationships and the will to use this understanding to manipulate people.

The Order and Fire elements might cross to create a type of story in which the protagonist's interests are frustrated and they become a creature of rage, never getting what they feel they were promised.

It might also mean that they get exactly what they want and they end the story triumphant.

| SILVER | CREATION | EARTH |

41. Silver and Creation and Earth

The elements of Creation and Earth suggest a peaceful advance of some kind into the future, and the element of Silver might suggest that this occurs in an intellectual field, like a science.

This combination might suggest a futuristic science fiction story in which the bounties of progress have increased the standard of living or material wealth.

A person grows up wondering about all kinds of questions and what they mean for him and for other people, and after some apparently random encounters meets a group of people who welcome him as one of their own.

This group could be a secret society, an alien race or shamen living in a higher dimension of reality.

The protagonist might have to do or cause any number of bizarre things to draw the attention of this group of people, some of whom might not even be human.

Drawing their attention could also be the mere beginning of the story, as there may be initiatory tests or missions to complete once the protagonist advances.

SILVER　CREATION　WATER

42. Silver and Creation and Water

With the elements of Creation and Water there is an image of people creating romance or love out of nothing, or out of an unlikely circumstance.

The element of Silver might represent this romance being related to social climbing of some kind.

Perhaps a guy goes to university to advance socially, meets an upper middle class girl and they hit it off, or a woman finally meets the composed, educated gentleman she always needed to feel complete.

The protagonist and their love interest might initially appear to be very poorly matched, or there might be some massive initial impediment to their forming a relationship.

In this sort of story they could keep falling in with each other as if fated to be together. Perhaps there is a comic series of denials or misunderstandings before this fate becomes clear to both parties.

This could also be a love at first sight type of story in which the protagonists became strongly attracted from the very beginning, and fate interrupted to keep them apart.

43. Silver and Creation and Air

The elements of Silver and Air suggest a mental advancement or knowledge of some kind.

A man's curiosity about the natural world leads him to become a scientist, and through the people he meets in this occupation he gains a valuable insight about how people or the world operate.

Perhaps he comes upon a theory that explains much of human behaviour, or a rule of thumb that is valuable because it suggests the opposite of what is apparent.

The element of Creation might represent the thought-form that the man creates as he comes to understand this aspect of humanity.

This type of story could take many outcomes depending on how this intellectual power was used.

The protagonist could popularise his insights and allow human understanding to advance, benefiting large numbers of people. He could also keep his wisdom to themselves because the vast majority of people cannot or should not be made to fathom such secrets.

SILVER CREATION FIRE

44. Silver and Creation and Fire

The elements of Creation and Fire suggest a great power that, when kindled, could take any number of paths.

A woman learns that a sensual art she has mastered gives her the power to captivate high society. Perhaps she is a dancer or courtesan of some unusual talent, leading her to rise in the world of politics by taking the ear of many influential men over the course of her life.

This type of story could be set in a number of different times and places, as much of the nature of politics is universal. It could easily be a speculative fiction setting.

If it was, it might be a fantasy in which the protagonist travelled far and through many different cultures and lands, sometimes as a spy or a trader of some kind.

The protagonist could also be a male who had attained a high level of skill in some valuable ability, perhaps music.

This type of story might stay very open-ended because of the Creation and Fire combination, and so might suit a format such as a series of short stories or a multiverse, in which some characters and themes reoccurred.

SILVER | DESTRUCTION | EARTH

45. Silver and Destruction and Earth

The elements of Destruction and Silver here suggest a loss of social place, of pride or of some other status.

A poet on the battlefield recounts his thoughts during the fighting, and how they led him to an appreciation of the peaceful life he returned to. The element of Silver comes through in his having achieved a higher perspective on his problems.

This could also be a story about a person lost on a desert island, removed from all of the social structures that they relied upon.

Such a person might discover a lot of things about themselves or about the world if all of their social networks were suddenly destroyed. This could be done through physical or mental isolation.

Physical isolation might involve getting stuck in the wilderness, trapped in a house or even in prison.

Mental isolation might involve a phobia or paranoia that keeps a person detached from other people, or stops them from feeling any warmth from human contact.

46. Silver and Destruction and Water

The combination of Water, Destruction and Silver suggests a story about love and war told from the perspective of someone high up in it, like an officer.

A war nerd becomes an officer and discovers while in battle that there's a human side to the conflict that he failed to appreciate. Broken and repentant, he finds a woman who respects his change of heart and marries him.

A woman tasked with a diplomatic mission finds herself caught up in a collapse of civilisation brought on by a civil war. In the chaos she meets a striking man who is calm in the chaos and they fall for each other.

Either kind of protagonist might find that their romantic interest provided some sort of balance to the person the protagonist had become.

The love story could naturally develop from the circumstances or it could hinder the progress of the protagonist in achieving their goals.

If the latter, an interesting character dilemma can develop if the protagonist finds themselves torn between two sides.

SILVER | DESTRUCTION | AIR

47. Silver and Destruction and Air

The combination of Silver and Air suggests a story that takes its drama mostly from the social aspect of the protagonist's life.

A man from the country travels to the city to take up a new position, and after meeting some of his colleagues comes to understand that his knowledge of animal interaction gives him a considerable advantage when it comes to office and local politics.

It could be that he has a special insight when it comes to the sort of territory and dominance games that animals play, and so is naturally skilled at avoiding such conflicts at work.

If his position involved a political aspect from the beginning (perhaps he is a member of Parliament for some rural constituency) he may find himself bound for high office.

The element of Destruction would come through in the damage that was done to him and to the people he encountered because of the nature of his position. There could be vicious rivalries, treachery and backstabbing of all kinds, and much of it unavoidable.

48. Silver and Destruction and Fire

The combination of Silver and Fire suggests a story about rulership and control; this, combined with Destruction, suggests a brutal and treacherous political story.

A man tries to ingratiate himself with the local powermongers. Possibly this is a story about the behind the scenes machinations of politics.

He could find himself involved in some shady deal that compromised his reputation in the business, or even a criminal arrangement that a number of people had to keep silent about.

Perhaps the arrangements don't work out so well for the protagonist and they are what is destroyed in the story. It could also be that the protagonist is tasked with doing the destroying, whether of an enemy or of their reputation.

This type of story affords a lot of scope for a twisting tale of intrigue, in which the protagonist sometimes acts in accord with others and sometimes alone. Possibly if it was a political story the protagonist would not know themselves exactly who was on the side of who, adding to the dramatic tension.

49. Gold and Chaos and Earth

In contrast to the other stories so far, the element of Gold here suggests a story about a person who takes on a righteous or spiritual struggle.

Elements of Chaos and Earth suggest a story that starts with the whole world being turned upside down, and ending happily.

The basic archetype of this story involves a moral crusader who goes into battle against, and defeats, a hated oppressive enemy, destroying it and bringing peace to the kingdom.

This type of story could be a more personal one in which an individual overcomes a personal demon like an old bitterness, addiction or delusion.

If it is, the golden character of the protagonist might shine forth at some point to cast out those inner problems or to light the way forward.

If the story needs an element of Chaos in order to get started, this could mean that the Gold nature of the protagonist wasn't immediately obvious, and only became so as the story required it.

50. Gold and Chaos and Water

The element of Water, when crossed with Gold, might not mean a romantic engagement but a spreading of succour and goodwill throughout the world.

This type of story could be about a group of doctors or peacemakers who travel into a war zone. Despite the chaos around them they are able to bring healing and peace to the people they encounter.

If the theme was idealistic, there could be a number of ups and downs during the course of the story as the characters struggled with disappointment and disillusionment.

As with all of the stories involving protagonists of Gold, much of the outcome of the story will be determined by whether or not that character benefits from their good nature.

If the protagonist benefits in this kind of story it could be because the love and peace they bring has a lasting positive effect on the people they touched. If the story is to take a more tragic tone, the protagonist's efforts might come to nothing as fate or an evil will come to counter them.

51. Gold and Chaos and Air

The combination of Chaos and Air suggests a very whimsical story, and crossed with Gold this might be a good-natured one.

It could be a comedy about a nice person who can't find anyone who needs their help. Perhaps they are very kind and very much want to be of use to someone but there just doesn't seem to be any need for such a person as them.

The element of Air might involve them being blown about to different places and peoples looking for a place to fit.

Some of the comedy element might involve the character of Gold temporarily becoming other character types in response to the frustrations they encounter, such as Iron if they become angry or Clay if they became despondent.

Because Gold is subtly transformed by the gentle Air, this story could involve some very subtle humour.

This type of story is perhaps one of the most chaotic and free-flowing, and there might be a lot of room for surprising the reader with strange twists and turns.

GOLD   CHAOS   FIRE

52. Gold and Chaos and Fire

The elements of Gold crossed with Fire and Chaos suggest that a theme of Gold melting away.

Perhaps it is a tragedy in which a person's good nature caused them to be too soft to succeed in a certain challenge.

It could also be a story about false gold; the melting is a melting away of a facade that reveals something much less valuable underneath. This aspect could be a revelation a character receives or one about that character.

If the former, the protagonist might realise that a person in their life or a group of people aren't as good as the protagonist thought they were. Perhaps some incident occurs and the protagonist sees an aspect of behaviour they had not expected.

If the latter, it could be that someone gets a clearer picture of the protagonist. The protagonist may or may not be aware that they were creating a false impression.

It could also be that the false impression is of some other element, and the Chaos and Fire strip that element back to reveal the Gold beneath.

GOLD **ORDER** **EARTH**

53. Gold and Order and Earth

The combination of Gold and Order suggests everything being or becoming the way it ought to be, and the element of Earth suggests that this is an enduring quality in the story.

It might not be easy finding an avenue for creative drama in a story in which everything goes well, but there is always a potential balance to be struck and thus a possible collapse into chaos if things are working out unacceptably well.

This type of story could be about an angel that came down to Earth to help set things right. Perhaps the dramatic conflict already exists in the story world and the protagonist of this type of story comes to fix it.

The elements of Order and Earth might imply a kind of stagnation, forcing the character of Gold to rebel against it, and so they bring freedom and happiness to the people in the story world.

This type of story could also be about the kind of self-actualisation concerns that strike people whose lives are generally without pressing need. This would include boredom and existential loneliness and angst.

54. Gold and Order and Water

The elements of Gold and Water suggest a beautiful love that may heal someone. Crossed with the element of Order, this brings an image of calming down an unpleasant feeling or mood.

This type of story could be a comedy about a woman who cannot get herself together emotionally and is inspired towards self-improvement by meeting a man she desires. Eventually she discovers the love of herself she needed to stay stable.

A male protagonist in a similar situation might find he is also challenged by needing to demonstrate a good nature in order to impress his romantic interest.

In any story like this, the elements of Water and Order might suggest an element of self-healing that must take place before the story can reach a satisfactory conclusion.

This could mean that the protagonist does not start as a character of Gold but must become one. It could also mean that they were a character of Gold but fell into a darker state for some reason.

GOLD | ORDER | AIR

55. Gold and Order and Air

The elements of Gold and Order suggest a story dynamic that is based around things being put right; the element of Air brings with it an aspect of a great intellectual or psychological insight.

This could be a story about a Chosen One coming to the world. A person with incredible spiritual insight comes to the world and is soon considered divine.

The story might be best if written from the perspective of someone who gets caught up in the dramas that this spiritual being naturally creates as they interact with the world.

The protagonist could be a character tasked with keeping the person of insight out of trouble, or perhaps interpreting their wisdom to be understood by a wider audience.

On a more individual level, this could be a story about a great insight that a person has about their own lives. The protagonist might have an epiphany that defines a large part of their approach to the world.

The drama might then come from the challenges the protagonist has in applying this wisdom to better themselves.

56. Gold and Order and Fire

The elements of Gold and Fire might combine here to suggest a moral power of some kind. The element of Order might refer to the vast reach of this power - vast enough to apply its own order to the world.

This type of story could be about a righteous new religious order, or perhaps a spiritual one.

A new movement of religious believers rises up and takes control of several major political offices. As individuals across the world become transformed by this new belief, so too does society and culture change.

If the story was more of a dystopia, the religious order might become a theocracy that stifles human expression and joy. The protagonist might then find themselves tasked with infiltrating and attacking this order, perhaps by pretending to be one of them.

Perhaps inevitably, if there was a religious element to this story there would also be a grand cataclysmic end battle. This might happen if an infiltration was discovered and the organisation fell into civil war, or if an opposing force gathered enough strength to challenge it.

GOLD CREATION EARTH

57. Gold and Creation and Earth

The elements of Creation and Earth suggest something material that comes into being, and the element of Gold brings an image of this being a good thing that is desired.

Perhaps it is a magic talisman of some kind that when touched offers healing or a supernatural gift.

If the object created is too good, or too valuable, it might be fought over. If a number of different parties became aware of its existence at the same time they might contest for possession of the magic item.

The protagonist of this type of story might be innocently caught up in all of this seeking, perhaps because they possess the magic item and are not aware of it.

They might also be a hero tasked with making sure that an evil force does not take control of the item.

There could be a wider conflict around such an item if it was extremely powerful. An object that was capable of bringing power to nations might be the sort of thing that world-ending wars were fought over.

GOLD   CREATION   WATER

58. Gold and Creation and Water

The elements of Gold and Water suggest a healing endeavour, and the element of Creation suggests an ability that is used to make this happen.

In this type of story, a person might heal another's sickness through the application of correct compassion.

Perhaps they are the lover that another character needed to heal their wounded soul. The protagonist might find that meeting this person gives them the chance to love again and with this come vast changes in their outlook and approach to life.

The element of Creation could come through in that the protagonist and their love interest build some sort of life together.

Because this type of story is so pleasant, and is such a common story type, it might be necessary to add a number of twists to it in order to make it unique and interesting.

Perhaps the protagonist is be in the middle of a prolonged period of despair when they meet their love interest, and need to be awakened from it.

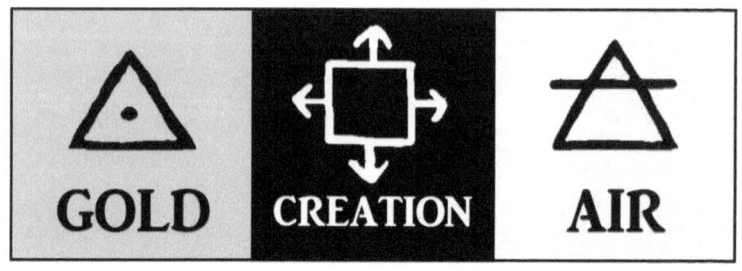

GOLD | CREATION | AIR

59. Gold and Creation and Air

Crossing Gold and Air suggests some high-minded, humanitarian endeavour, and these crossed with Creation suggest the building of an organisation or movement that is tasked with furthering this.

For a longer story, it might be more interesting if the protagonist joined such an enterprise at a low level. Then they could progress up the ranks through all the dramas that would inevitably arise from life in such a movement.

The humanitarian endeavour that forms the backdrop of the story could be one that works properly or one that doesn't. If the latter, the protagonist may find themselves in a number of dilemmas as they try and bring order out of chaos in their worklife.

Over the course of the story, the protagonist will have to form a number of different parties of allies as they try to keep themselves safe from infiltrators and to navigate the currents of fortune.

Because of the element of Creation in this story, the movement in it might get larger and larger, propelling the protagonist into ever more epic and dramatic situations.

GOLD　CREATION　FIRE

60. Gold and Creation and Fire

The combination of Gold and Fire here suggests some sort of righteous power, and the element of Creation might suggest the ability to bring this power into being.

The powers in this story could be symbolised by an object of power. This could be a talisman of magic power or even the sceptre to a kingdom.

The elements in this story suggest the creation of such a power, rather than fighting over one. It could be a story about the formation of a kingdom out of a number of tribes, and backed by some righteous power that brings learning and enlightenment to the world.

As a dramatic element this process might occur after a major war or during some other period of darkness. The protagonist would then aid in bringing people cautiously out of a dark age.

The opposition in this type of story might come from barbarians, from evil forces within, or from the ignorance and superstition of one character that leads the group to disaster. Tasked with bringing light to the world, the protagonist could face direct conflict with any kind of dark force.

GOLD   DESTRUCTION   EARTH

61. Gold and Destruction and Earth

This type of story could be about a Gold that drives out all opposition and creates a new holy order.

The protagonist of this story might find themselves swept up in a wider social movement that brought a new kind of enlightenment to the world in the ashes of the old one. This would make this a story about revolution and a new beginning,

This could twist into a very cruel dystopia, in which only people of a perceived quality were allowed to have certain rights.

Such a dark possibility might become a reality if the forces of Gold were suffocated after a time of being in charge, or if they became corrupted somehow.

Perhaps this type of story carries with it tones of hope, renewal and justice. If the protagonist is the character of Gold they may find themselves actively fighting to counter the will of the old order.

This type of story is perhaps more concerned with the aftermath than with the revolution.

GOLD · DESTRUCTION · WATER

62. Gold and Destruction and Water

The elements of Destruction and Water suggest a romantic tragedy of some kind, or a love story that draws energy from some kind of destruction.

This type of story could be a simple romance about an attraction formed after some righteous destruction. Perhaps the protagonist observes another character's outrage and action and falls for their strength and courage.

The protagonist might see the other character as a force for good fighting against an enemy in an unfair world.

It could also be a tragedy about a kind but naive person who ended up being destroyed by falling in love with the wrong person.

Perhaps because of their kindness they were induced to only see the good side of a person who turned out to be more complicated.

A twist on this may be that the thing destroyed is the bad part of the romantic partner. It could have been an element of themselves that they did not like and the romance gives them the chance to discard it.

63. Gold and Destruction and Air

The combination of Destruction and Air suggests something being gently erased or worn away.

This might reveal a layer of Gold underneath. Perhaps through repeated batterings and discouragements a character of Gold rises up and takes their place.

A less pleasant version of this type of story might involve an element of Gold being gently worn away or destroyed. This might occur if a character of Gold was subjected to such repeated losses that they gave up.

Either of these types of story could be replicated on a wider level for a more epic scope. The former might involve a people who came together in response to some threat from the natural environment, such as a severe storm or a flood.

The latter might be a story about the slow failure and falling apart of a colony due to starvation or disease.

Because Gold is the softest element, beautiful things can be created with the gentlest input. This type of story could also reflect a sculpture of some kind, in that parts were slowly removed to make the whole look more beautiful.

64. Gold and Destruction and Fire

The combination of Destruction and Fire suggest a dark tone to this story, and this crossed with an element of Gold suggests a tragedy befalling a decent person.

A man who society sees as high-ranking realises that all his work is worthless and destroys it in a fit of rage.

It could be that the work failed to lead him to his ultimate goal or that his obsession with it caused him to lose something he loved.

This type of story could also be about a person's destruction from libel or rumour. The Gold might represent the goodwill that people have towards them which is destroyed by the gossiping.

The central theme to a story like this could be despair, as the destructive forces burn up all hope of a positive resolution. This might make the protagonist feel as if they were very unlucky or even cursed.

It could also represent a kind of resolution, as the character of Gold demonstrated their higher understanding by persevering through terrible destruction.

INVENTING YOUR OWN ARCHETYPES

All of the story ideas and patterns described in this book have been derived from a simple archetypal matrix.

In essence, it consists of three dimensions, with the first being character class, the second being situation energy and the third outcome feeling. Each of these dimensions has four point, and four times four times four is sixty-four.

This is by no means the only way to derive sixty-four basic story types from three abstract, arbitrary dimensions. Any or all of the three dimensions given in this book could be changed for something else.

For example, the character class element in this book that is represented by the elements of Clay, Iron, Silver and Gold could reflect a personality element such as a combination of two of the four dichotomies on the Myers-Briggs Type Indicator.

In this way, extraverted and thinking might stand in for Clay, extraverted and feeling for Iron, introverted and thinking for Silver and introverted and feeling for Gold.

If you wanted some stock characters it would be as simple as declaring that Clay = young woman, Iron = young man, Silver = old woman, Gold = old man.

The story situations could likewise be altered so that the

four points fell on a different dimension to story energy.

The second dimension could easily be a moral dimension, with the protagonist either good or evil, or becoming better or becoming worse.

Likewise, the four points along the dimension of story outcome could be changed to anything else.

If writing a battle story, they could relate instead to the strategic outcome, so that Earth = heavy loss, Water = loss, Air = victory, Fire = major victory.

When using archetypes in this manner, it is possible to get both ideas for plot developments and for interesting character conflicts.

In principle there is no limit to the number of archetypes that can be chosen to get an idea of the energy behind a story. This book offers only one possible way of doing so.

Also by VJM Publishing:

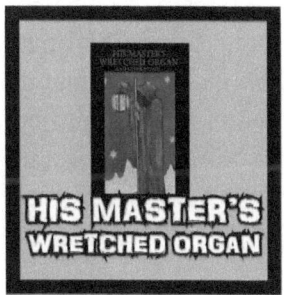

His Master's Wretched Organ is a collection of short stories that probe themes of disconnection, self-inquiry, spiritual ascendancy, awe and horror.

The Verity Key is a New Zealand cyberpunk novel about a young virtual reality fighting champion who finds himself drawn into the saga of a device that can control the thoughts of other people by satellite.

Learn Spanish Vocabulary With Mnemonics uses mnemonics to teach Spanish vocabulary as quickly and efficiently as possible. Some of the mnemonics are weird, some sexy, some cheerfully obscene, but all are memorable.

The *Cannabis Activist's Handbook* is a book for people interested in cannabis law reform. It consists of three parts, one about building a cannabis law reform movement, one about winning the arguments for cannabis law reform and one about taking the fight to the streets.

Stop Smoking Cigarettes With the Token Economy Method describes how a smoker can use a cognitive behavioural therapy method called the Token Economy to stop smoking cigarettes.

The Book of Faith is a satirical book about honest ways to accrue faith in the modern religious marketplace.

www.ingramcontent.com/pod-product-compliance
Lightning Source LLC
Chambersburg PA
CBHW050505290526
45786CB00006B/2449